The 10 Habits of Successful Real Estate Investors

Malcolm Silver

Thanks to the Creative team:

Jody Samuels
Jill Battson

The 10 Habits of Successful Real Estate Investors

Published by:
90-Minute Books
302 Martinique Drive
Winter Haven, FL 33884
www.90minutebooks.com

Published in the United States of America

ISBN-13: 978-0692603765
ISBN-10: 069260376X

For more information on 90-Minute Books including finding out how you can publish your own lead generating book, visit www.90minutebooks.com or call (863) 318-0464

Here's What's Inside…

Introduction

When I meet with people who want to invest in real estate, their vision of what it entails is often very different from the reality. One of the reasons that I love this business is that there are so many complex layers – but it's not for everyone.

At first glance, investing in real estate seems to be a very simple endeavour, but it's really not. When you drill down, there's a lot to consider. I wanted to write a book so that people who are considering investing, but don't know where to start, would have a guide. This book is based on habits that took me years to hone, and which make my own real estate investments successful.

Over the years I have created 10 habits that evolved as my own experience grew – a combination of cataloguing my successes and failures, listening to successful mentors and immersing myself in the business. I've gone out of my way to learn what successful real estate investors do and how they do it. By watching and listening, I saw that there was a pattern to their habits, and gradually I adopted and finessed my own habits based on what I saw. I use the habits every day in my business and they are the foundation to my success.

I hope this book inspires you to create your own habits and dive into the business of real estate investing.

To your success!

Malcolm Silver

Why aren't more people successful real estate investors?

Investing in real estate is like investing in anything. You have to know what you're doing, and most importantly, you must be prepared to do the work. Investing in real estate is not as simple as people might expect, because they are usually trying to buy a sizeable asset and the amount of money is generally a significant amount for most people to invest.

Therefore, successful real estate investment is not something that a person can do quickly and easily; it will be tough - which can be problematic for people busy with another profession. Generally, if people are unsure of what they are doing, they get nervous and don't take the plunge. This book will help people get a better understanding of what it takes to successfully invest in real estate.

Toronto!

In my home city of Toronto, real estate is booming. One of the factors driving this current upswing is the long-awaited creation of an additional subway line, which will run across the mid-town section of the city. The City of Toronto hasn't added to their subway lines in 60 years. Historically, investment in transit was poorly managed. However, the increase in transit will promote growth in real estate development, especially along the proposed subway route and main streets of the city. It will help transform bleak and run-down areas and bring life into them. I've seen this pattern in other cities and it will be the same in Toronto.

Other contributing factors to the boom include: the increase of immigration, the rise of Toronto as the financial centre of Canada, and new high tech companies, like Google and Uber who are calling Toronto home.

Toronto's City planners are looking forward to this transformation. They would like to see the main avenues of Toronto become high-rise corridors, like Manhattan, which will make it easier for people to travel the city streets, as well as to shop, live and work. Toronto is estimated to grow by 100,000± people a year and they all can't move to the suburbs, and neither do they want to; the city must densify.

My business is exclusively acquisition of commercial real estate. I know people who only purchase residential properties and they love it, but the only residential tenants I deal with are the ones who live above my commercial properties. Because

I only have a small number of residential apartments I am able to renovate them into desirable living spaces, which attracts good tenants and leads to buildings that give a good return on investment.

Toronto's boom certainly encourages people to think they can make money in real estate. The boom also attracts international buyers who are investing in residential properties. They buy condos by the block, and this type of investor will not be interested in the commercial properties that I acquire. My work is too management-intense. Typically, these international investors are moving their money out of their own - sometimes volatile - countries. To some extent they represent a threat to investors like me because they don't care a great deal about the return as their key motivation is preserving their capital in a safe and stable country. Generally though, this trend hasn't really affected me because I like to keep my operation small and personal, but I have heard from the larger Canadian investment groups that they are definitely being hurt by this trend. They're finding that the overseas investors are driving down the returns and are making it difficult for the local buyers.

The Upside to Real Estate Investing

In my opinion, real estate is the only logical and sensible investment. As long as Toronto continues to grow, real estate here will continue to be a good investment. Capital gains can be very significant and are far superior to any other forms of investing. Nobody has control over the stock market and it can crash leaving you with next to nothing.

Some people put their money into a Real Estate Investment Trust, (REIT), which are typically well managed, but you will have no idea what kind of fees you will be charged, or exactly what buildings you are buying into.

To me, it's a unique feeling being a real estate owner. I prefer property ownership to the stock market, or to simply putting money in the bank, or under the mattress, because I enjoy being actively involved in my investments. The day-to-day challenges of real estate keep me active. It's exciting looking for new properties, caring for and improving the buildings and seeking new partners with whom to invest.

Typically, real estate investment provides a much better return than the stock market. Compared to my few stocks, I've seen my capital grow dramatically with some of the properties I own and I like feeling like I have some control over my destiny.

The 10 Habits of Successful Real Estate Investors

As I mentioned before, as soon as I started in this business I realized that to be successful – in any business, really – takes commitment, time and energy. Developing good habits help bring a focus to whatever you are doing.

As you read on I will explain the 10 habits that have made me successful.

Habit #1: Invest in Real Estate for the Right Reasons

What are some of the reasons that people think are the right ones for choosing real estate investments?

The first reason is if you are prepared to make a long-term commitment - somewhere between five and ten years of having your money tied up. If you invest with a view toward capital gains rather than income, then I believe that's a good reason, as well. If people want short-term returns, real estate is a waste of time, unless you're interested in flipping properties. Sometimes you can receive an attractive offer to cash out within two years, but that is unusual.

Another reason, and equally important, is that you have to want to do it. Ideally, you will have an affinity for architecture, or people's lifestyles. If you look around and see the tremendous development in the city at the moment, you'll know that the city is changing; real estate will be a major part of that change – and a good investment.

Other reasons are that it offers an independent life style if you invest in a big way, or you might be looking for an opportunity to supplement a part time job, both to enjoy more income and for job satisfaction.

Investors may keep all their money in the stock market or in the bank. Why not diversify and put a portion of your money in real estate? Not only is investment in real estate so important in the growth of Toronto but we have also seen great successes in real estate investing over the last 20 or 30 years.

If you want liquid assets that you can quickly convert, then owning real estate is not a good choice.

Habit #2: Complete Your Education with a Mentor

Successful people, in any field, engage mentors at various points in their careers to help them learn and grow. Even if you are confident that you can go it alone, occasional contact with a mentor can shift you out of being locked into your own head and your own ideas.

I learnt real estate by talking to other real estate investors who were successful. I asked them questions: "What do I have to do and what do I look for?" Over time, if you're dealing with the right people, they can teach you a lot. The more that you learn and the faster you learn it, the easier it's going to be for you; otherwise, you will have to teach yourself, which is usually a long and painful / expensive process. I sought out mentors and the best way to approach things. If you can, read biographies about people who have been successful investors; learn from them about what they have done. Usually these books are a compelling read.

The other way to go is to find a professional investing coach. Some of the things you'll have to decide are how often you want to communicate with them, what kind of personality you would like – aggressive or gentle, how much you are prepared to pay for the service, and if the coach has a track record that inspires you with confidence.

Choose an investing coach who can act as a mentor, who is experienced and successful at investing. You may just want to meet with someone on an informal basis from time to time and talk through your problems. Currently, there is a new course at the University of Toronto that allows people to study real estate and real estate investing. Those professors could certainly act as coaches, and the course itself could be done at night but it's not really something you need to study formally.

Instead, attend conferences, trade shows, seminars, investing groups and webinars and read everything you can that pertains to the kind of real estate you're interested in.

Learning to invest really is much more difficult to do on your own. If you decide to go it alone, instead of seeking a mentor, but you will have to be much more focused and design strategies of accountability with yourself. It's just a great deal easier to do it with someone else who knows. Why re-invent the wheel?

Habit #3: Complete an Investor's Business Plan

If you want to be a serious investor then you need to do it professionally, and treat it like embarking on any other kind of business - which means committing, in writing, what you want to do, how you want to do it and set some deadlines.

Before you start writing the plan, think generally about the types of properties you might like to acquire, the amount of money you'd be comfortable investing and how you would like to allocate those funds. Whether you will manage the property yourself or find a professional team with whom you will feel comfortable. Once you write down your plans it becomes a concrete commitment to becoming a professional investor in real estate.

I can't stress enough the importance of knowing what kind of property you prefer because the real estate industry is very diverse. You can't dabble in everything. You can't buy a house, buy apartments, and buy land. They're all separate areas with their own quirks. You have to decide what you like - and what you think you might like.

After you have the first thought about what/when/where, get a pen and paper, or open a Word document on your computer, and make some hard decisions why you need or want to do it.

Since there are a lot of things to be done, it's important that you put down all of these details in writing, and then you can start to see what you're getting into.

It's not just about finding a property and buying it. Investors have to learn to focus. With real estate, you've got to focus on one or two particular niches, or one or two areas. It's impossible to do everything, everywhere, at the same time.

I prefer to restrict myself to areas a radius of one hour's drive from the office. I stick to neighbourhoods of Toronto that I consider to be up and coming. I don't want to start flying back and forth to see properties, mainly because I enjoy meeting people and dealing with problems in person.

I've laid out some of the steps you might want to consider as you start to write your business plan:

1. Identify your objective: Are you investing for the short term (1 – 3 years) or long term (5 – 20).

2. What are your financial expectations: Are you buying property to create an increase in your equity/real estate wealth, or are you buying to create a stream of income that you can use to live on or retire on?

3.What type of property are you interested in buying: Which properties will best fulfill your objectives? Residential? Typically houses or apartment buildings. Commercial? Usually a retail store with apartments above. Or industrial? Typically a warehouse or factory.

4. Identify how you will go about finding investment properties: Will you enjoy searching for properties yourself or would it be better to find an agent to help you. Another option is to find investors who are selling units in limited partnerships investing in properties that you like.

5. Identify your investment criteria: What kind of return are you looking for and how much borrowing can you tolerate.

6. Identify how much money you would like to invest, or how much money you are prepared to borrow.

7. Will you manage the property yourself or hire a company to manage it for you? If you decide to manage it yourself, you'll need a team of tradespeople necessary to both renovate and repair the property. These include: plumber, roofer, electrician, contractor, handyman, cleaner, painter, door and window supplier and locksmith.

8. Identify areas of the city that interest you: Do you want properties on the main street with visibility, or are you happy to be in a suburb or centre with less visibility? Do you favour new buildings in perfect condition, or old buildings that may well be run down and in need of renovation? The best way to identify the neighbourhood that is right for you is to walk the streets both in the daytime and at night. Have a coffee with the locals, go into the stores and chat to people about their neighbourhood.

9. Where will your financing come from? Will you easily be able to line up debt financing from your bank, trust company or mortgage broker?

10. Identify how you will manage the accounting. Will this new investment impact your personal financial situation and do you have a real estate lawyer as part of your team?

Habit #4: Build a Team

Build a team by knowing all of the different kinds of people that you must deal with to make a successful real estate investment. That's where your business plan can clarify your thoughts. You find your team either by trial and error or by asking for recommendations from other people who are in the business.

Real Estate Agent: You'll need an agent who has proven experience at finding the sort of properties that you are interested in buying. Be very careful in the selection of your agent and make 100% sure that he really has substantial commercial experience and not just residential experience because the two fields are completely different. There is more to learn about a commercial property than there is about buying a house. Also ask what properties he likes to buy.

Lawyer: You'll need a lawyer who has substantial and varied experience in the type of real estate transactions you are contemplating. Your lawyer will also deal with the zoning so you will know what the building can be used for today and in the future.

Financing: Ability to finance a project is so key it needs to be put in place prior to making an offer on a property if possible. You will need to find out from your bank if they are interested in lending you the money for your contemplated investment. If your bank cannot or will not lend you money for this transaction, then you will need to find a mortgage broker who can arrange the financing for you.

Contractor: You'll need an experienced contractor who is flexible and can handle the kinds of repairs, renovations and possible problems you may encounter.

Appraiser: To obtain financing from a bank you will have to arrange an appraisal by someone recognized and acceptable to the lending institution.

Inspector: You'll need to have a qualified property inspector to examine the property as part of your due diligence. He will examine every aspect of how the property is functioning and can alert you to possible areas of danger and expense.

My team has come about by a combination of referrals and chance encounters. You'll need quite a large team when you're buying something and running it properly. Of course, you'll need an accountant to prepare your financial statements.

Choose your team carefully because these people can really help or hinder you dramatically.

I can't stress enough how absolutely vital it is that you have a good lawyer because there are so many pitfalls, so many things that can go wrong, and to watch for, when you buy a property or create a lease.

Habit #5: Define Your Goals

When contemplating investing seriously in real estate it is vital that you sit down and think very clearly about your goals, because what your goals are will influence a lot of your decisions.

One of your goals may be to earn a certain amount of money each year. Perhaps you are interested in building equity for the long term.

Other goals may be to build a team around you and to create a serious real estate investment company. In the process, you may want to obtain a real estate agent's license.

You may want to create income by flipping properties. Or your goals might be a combination of these.

I defined my goals at the beginning. I wanted to combine earning a sum of income each year, which would increase over a five year period, and amassing a certain dollar number of gross assets each year, culminating in a grand total goal by 2020.

Habit #6: Choose a Niche

When you hear a person say, "I want to invest in real estate," you have to ask: "In which real estate do you want invest? Do you want to buy apartments or a commercial property? Do you want to buy a house or land or an industrial property? Do you want to buy something that's brand new, or just in great shape? Are you prepared to buy something that's a mess and turn it around?"

These are questions you have to ask yourself that will determine your 'niche'. After that, you will also need to decide what property and investment you like and your comfort level with it, as well as what you can reasonably afford and your estimation of a sensible plan for you to start. It's personal; you've just got to figure that out for yourself.

I don't think it's sensible to say, "I'll look at everything." I buy run-down commercial properties in rising areas near transit, that's my niche. Other people like to buy brand-new, commercial condos or apartment buildings. I can't give advice on identifying a good niche for you to start with, because this is a personal choice linked to defining your goals. You've got to decide what kind of property you want.

Typically, the rewards in real estate investment have gone to the patient and long-term minded people who know what their niche is. Rewards have also gone to the people that had the vision and the guts to buy something that nobody else would have wanted to touch, who turned it around, perhaps changed its use or re-zoned it, and made it into something great and more valuable.

The types of properties that I have bought were a very good place to begin for me because they didn't cost a fortune at the time I bought, and they were a very good way to cut my teeth and to learn how to do everything. My portfolio is filled with modest properties and now I'm ready to grow into much bigger properties. The problems that I will encounter with big properties are basically the same with more zeros attached.

Habit #7: Find a Good Deal

You have to watch the market cycle in the city you're investing in in order to find a good deal. Are you buying into a building in such a hot area that the prices probably cannot rise any higher than their current state? Are you buying in an area where nobody currently wants to go but where gentrification is taking place? Or somewhere there's a possibility of a future big zoning change? Have you started to notice key retail stores like Starbucks moving in or is there a new transit system-planned?

When you take these factors into consideration then you're ready to buy at a sensible price. Be prepared to do the renovations. The building could be completely run-down, or previously owned by amateur investors without money to renovate and who didn't care. If you see that by renovating the building to make it more attractive you will get a much better grade of tenant, then you'll want to do that. These things will ensure that your investment is sensible.

You have to believe in an area or in the kind of building that you're viewing, or you look at the condition of a building and know that you can dramatically improve it and/or change it.

Then, you've got to deal with the seller. You will want to try and gauge the enthusiasm of the seller - whether he is looking to retire and get out, or is desperate to sell because he is stretched financially. See what you can do to negotiate the price down, and don't be scared to put in a significantly lower bid than the asking price.

Before I make an offer on a building, I go through my numbers to work out what I think the price should be to make sense to the bottom line. I disregard the selling price completely, and work backwards. I work out the income that I can get out of the building and the amount that the building should be then worth, and then I look at the selling price. If there is a discrepancy, I'll offer the price that I feel is sensible.

But it doesn't work all the time. Unfortunately, the market in Toronto is very hot, so the sellers are arrogant and greedy. That makes it a difficult time to buy. Sometimes my offers are thrown out, but I just keep going. I'm not scared to offer what I consider to be the correct price, even if the seller considers the value to be significantly higher. Sometimes they'll respond, and sometimes they'll tell me to drop dead. You can't take it personally.

Habit #8: Use Other People's Money

One of the many beauties of real estate is that you don't have to have your own cash, or even all of the cash needed, to buy a building; you just need to have a portion, the down-payment or equity. Sometimes, you can even borrow that too.

For example, if you see a building you want to purchase and it costs a million dollars you don't have to reach into your cheque book and buy it outright. In fact it's better that you don't. Banks will typically lend you up to 70% of the money needed, so you've got to come up with the remaining 30%.

And keeping that 70% is crucial if you have to renovate, because it may be costly. You may not want to use your own money for renovation; you may want to borrow that as well from a bank that understands real estate. But if you do use your own money, and didn't use it all for the deposit, you will be able to start renovations straight away.

In the first year, you can put a short-term mortgage in place to finish renovating the building and lease it out. Then you can get the property appraised to show that it's worth much more than it was at the time when you bought it and then re-finance with a longer-term mortgage. That's value for your money!

Once the building is completely leased, your tenants are very kindly paying down the mortgage for you - so you don't even have to do that. Over time, the building will eventually become debt-free and owned by you outright, without you having had to pay for the majority of it.

Habit #9: Understand Cycles and be Patient

Real estate is a cyclical business. The cycles in the U.S. have typically happened every seven years. It's biblical, really. Historically, Toronto hasn't had cycles like that. The last dramatic crash in Toronto was in 1989, and the market has been steadily growing ever since, so we may be due for our major correction. It's just the nature of the beast and unavoidable. The market will go up and then go down, and then come back up again.

Certain cities in the U.S. have come back fairly quickly while other places have not. I can't tell you why it's like that but real estate can't keep going up forever. But the beauty of real estate is that no matter how far down it goes, even if you buy it at the peak and suddenly the price plunges, as long as you're prepared to wait and sit it out, it will eventually come back at a higher value than when you bought it. That's the virtue of patience.

To me, real estate is very much a long-term investment of five to ten years. When you look at the growth of real estate in Toronto, certainly over the last thirty years, it's just been amazing. As long as the city continues to grow, there's activity, and the place isn't falling apart, there will be growth and increase in value.

Habit #10: Measure your Performance

I use a pro-forma that shows all of the costs involved, the income that comes in, the expenses that the building incurs, the expenses that the tenant will take on, and my share of the expenses.

On-the pro-forma, I can see the rate of return, the return on cash, and also the value of the property at different return rates. I do that for every single property I'm interested in buying. I monitor the pro-forma because I own the properties. I've always got my original purchase price up on top so I can keep an eye on the value today and how the building is performing for me. That's how I measure my performance. It's very important to do it, and to do it constantly.

Every month, you've got to look at your numbers, watch your cash, and see how the building is doing. It's work. That's all. But it's very important.

The Myths of Real Estate Investing

The biggest myth of real estate investing is that you can't lose when you buy real estate. If you buy at the peak of the market and the market suddenly plunges, i.e. a mini-recession sets in and you can't get tenants, then suddenly your building is worth less. You'll get that awkward call from the bank and you could possibly lose a building.

Another big myth is that the key to successful real estate investing is three things - location, location, location. That's just not true at all. Timing could also replace those three words. Location is extremely important but you also have to buy at the right time and at the right price. If you're buying something beautiful in the hottest area but you're buying it at the peak price, it's probably not going to be a good investment. But if you're buying in a location that you feel is going to change dramatically for the better, then location is key.

As I mentioned previously, there is a cycle with real estate. You've got to watch that cycle. There's no point in buying in at the top when there is a big risk prices could plunge. We certainly saw that happen in the U.S. in 2008. It's a mistake to think it could never happen to you.

The Mistakes to Avoid When Investing in Real Estate

The biggest mistake investors can make is to buy the wrong kind of property in the wrong place at the wrong time. For example, buying a property that you can't manage yourself, or that is very difficult to manage, or it has nightmare tenants or is nearly falling down; that's certainly a recipe for disaster.

If you're buying in an area that has become fashionable and you're caught up in the frenzy of this wonderful area, you've got to step back and be very careful that you're not buying in at the top. If you buy at the top, you know what could happen next. Your property will probably go down not up in value.

Another big mistake is overpaying; you always have to be careful about that. Unfortunately, you don't really get to understand a lot about your investment until after you've bought the property. After a period of months or a year goes by, then you can see if, in fact, you paid a sensible price or not. That just comes with time.

Hopefully if you're buying a property with a tenant in place, it doesn't turn out to be a bad deal for you. That's a very serious mistake. If you don't do your research and find out that a tenant is lousy and doesn't pay rent, it causes a lot of trouble. Then you've got a real headache, because it is very difficult to evict a sitting tenant, especially if they're on a long-term lease. That's not fun.

The Advantages of Investing with a Team

If you invest on your own because you have the money and the wherewithal, and you've gathered your own team around you, then you control the whole project. You're answerable to nobody. That's the beauty of investing on your own and it's a definite advantage if you've got the time, the inclination, and the people around you.

I enjoy the challenges that come with management, but not everyone does. I especially like to be able to visit my properties in person at any time. All of my properties are within an hour's drive of my office so that I can be more hands-on with managing each building. I'm in control, more or less, and this is what I enjoy.

If you don't have that desire and you still want to own a piece of a building, then it's so much easier just to cut out all of the pain by working with somebody who's done it many times before, who knows exactly what to do, and whose strategy you trust and have confidence in. It's so much easier just to simply write a cheque, sit back, and then let someone else do all the work.

How to Invest in Real Estate the Right Way

If you don't have the desire to do it all yourself – either on your own, or by putting a team around you, then you can always invest with me.

Call and set up a meeting, so we can review what your goals and expectations are. I can explain the kinds of things that I do, and my process. We'll begin by taking a drive around town. I'll show you the kinds of properties that I have and where I have them, as well as the kinds of areas that I like to invest in.

I have developed a unique process called "The Investment Property Sourcing Advantage" This process enables prospective investors to understand exactly what I do and how I do it. Either they like my process, or they don't. If they want to go further with me, then they'll want to go out for a drive, or they won't. It's as simple as that.

In a partner I'm looking for people who are passive investors, who will just invest and leave everything to me. Sometimes an owner will want to partner with me on a project that could be an assembly of properties to be redeveloped into something new. In that case, I look to create a working relationship with the seller. I'm always looking for people who want to sell property and also people who want to invest with me.

I like investors who want an increase in capital gains, who believe in what I'm doing, and have confidence and trust in me.

In the course of work, I will often meet potential partners, such as people who have access to a property they would like to buy. Either they don't know how to buy it or can't do it on their own, so they call me and say, "Maybe you'd like to come in with me?" Typically, what I do are small syndications - less than 10 people per property with an average investment in the $50,000 - $100,000 range and like-minded investors focused on capital gains not income over a 5-10 year hold term.

Investment is not a game. Either you do it seriously or you don't do it at all.

Here's How to Invest in Real Estate with a Competitive Advantage.

Perhaps you've been thinking about investing in real estate for a while now, but you're not sure where to start or whether now is even the right time to invest.

That's where we come in. We help people just like you get a competitive advantage by helping-source and identify properties that will work for you and will provide a positive return.

Step 1: go to **www.MSilver.com** and fill out an online Investor Scorecard to assess your suitability to invest.

You can gain a competitive advantage by working with an experienced real estate investor who can help find the deals no one else is looking at.

If you'd like us to help, just send an email to: **malcolm@msilver.com** and we will take it from there.

Real Estate Jargon Clarified

In real estate, as in any industry, one often hears expressions—some slang, others simply odd—that neither the finest education nor the best dictionary is likely to illuminate. Understanding does not come with sunlight, so this informal guide explaining some of those uncommon terms will help.

Economic Terms

Capitalisation rate or cap rate A capitalisation rate is a short way of stating the yield /return that a buyer would receive by purchasing a property.

Example: if you wish to earn a 6 percent return on your investment, then you would have to buy at a forecasted 6 cap or higher. If a property is selling at a 7 cap, its buyer would receive a 7 percent return on that money.

Cap rates vary for many reason, ranging from the attributes of the property itself (location, vacancy rate, creditworthiness of its tenants, age of its roof, and so on), to interest rates or the economy as a whole.

The mathematical formula is simple, but it is easy to forget because the relationship between the purchase price and the cap rate is inverted. The investment price rises when the cap rate lowers and falls when the cap rate rises.

The formula is as follows: Cap rate equals purchase price divided by net-operating income (NOI) (expressed as a percentage). For example, assume NOI is $200,000. If the cap rate is 8, then the purchase price equals $2,500,000 ($200,000/.08).

Gross multiplier: This is another, simpler method for arriving at a price used in the sale of small apartment buildings. One takes the property's annual gross income and multiplies it by the agreed-upon gross multiplier. If the apartments gross $90,000 a year and if the gross multiplier is 10, then the price will be $900,000 ($90,000 x 10 = $900,000).

Internal rate of return, or IRR: The IRR is—in a perfect world—a method to determine an investor's total return from a property during the period of ownership, including both annual cash flow and ultimate sales proceeds. The calculation is neither simple nor without serious guesswork. One takes the projected annual cash flow that an investor hopes to receive from a property for a given period—usually ten years—and adds to that number the property's estimated sale value in the tenth year. The IRR is the percentage required to discount this combined sum back to zero on the date of purchase.

Example: if a property earns 5 percent in annual return over ten years and then sells at the end of that tenth year for twice what the investor originally paid for it, the IRR would be 10.98 percent. That is, to get all the cash coming in over the next ten years so you will have a net present value of zero today, you would have to discount it at 10.98 percent. Looked at positively, this result means you would have received a total return on your investment of 10.98 percent. Because this highly speculative 10.98 percent sounds much better than the 5 percent return you know you're getting from day one, the IRR is very popular.

The fallacy behind every IRR analysis is obvious; it requires one to predict the future so be wary.

Net operating income, or NOI: NOI has a widely held general meaning, but because it is the key of a property's value, its definition is subject to interpretation. Simply put, NOI is a property's annual gross rental income minus the property's—not the owner's—expenses for the same period.

The definition of "gross rental income" has relatively few pitfalls: whether to include (a) one-time payments (a lease termination fee) or (b) bank interest on deposits.

The definition of "expenses" can be more problematic. When one is defining NOI, expenses never include the owner's debt service or depreciation (i.e., the property is viewed as being free and clear of mortgages, and the tax situation is ignored). The debate begins after that: (a) what the management fee and vacancy factor should be; (b) whether and how much to include for reserves for future tenant improvements and leasing commissions, structural maintenance reserves, and roof replacement reserves; (c) how to handle capital repairs or improvements; and so on.

Flip: a verb meaning to sell a property at the same time one is purchasing it. With a signed purchase contract and a sufficiently long escrow period, a buyer of a property may, in a hot market, raise the price and secretly market it for resale before the buyer closes. The property is usually flipped to the second buyer at the same moment as the flipper's purchase, with the second buyer's money the only funds in escrow.

Lease Terms

Triple net: what a landlord strives for in a retail lease with the tenant paying absolutely all of a property's expenses. *Note*: even with a triple net lease, the landlord may have some unreimbursed expenses.

Base year: the year in which the landlord's share of a building's expenses for a particular tenant is established. It is usually the calendar year in which a lease starts or the 12-month period beginning when that tenant opens for business. In a base-year lease, the tenant pays costs but only to the extent they exceed base-year costs.

Definitions of area: *As* money is more important than math in the definition of a tenant's leased premises, the industry standards are subject to negotiation.

Gross leasable area, or GLA: the standard for retail leasing of "outside wall to outside wall," means that the GLA is the entire building or space with no deductions. Occasionally, the measurements are from the inside of the perimeter walls. Industrial buildings are also often leased on a gross square footage basis.

Net rentable area: an office leasing term that—assuming one were leasing an entire floor of a building—would be the standard for the leased premises. It is generally understood to be the total floor area less "vertical penetrations." Elevators, utility ducts, and staircases are the most readily agreed-upon verticals. Net rentable area includes all the floor's common areas if the floor contained more than one tenant. Such common areas would include the elevator lobby, the hallways, and the restrooms.

Net useable area: a calculation usually applied to multitenant floors in an office building. Net useable area is the net rentable area minus the common areas. Each tenant leases its pro rata share of the net useable area and a pro rata share of the deducted common areas. This calculation is called a *load factor*. Depending on the efficiency of the floor plate / floor and the relative bargaining strength of landlord and tenant, the load factor can vary wildly, but an average load seems to be about 10–12 percent.

Gross: a lease where the landlord pays all costs (including janitorial and utilities) without reimbursement from the tenant.

Go dark: in retail, a term that means powerful tenants insist on the right to close their business or go dark at any time (without, however, terminating the lease or any of its other obligations)

Percentage rent: If a retail tenant is compelled to grant rent increases, all but the most successful prefer it to be in the form of percentage rent. The rate or percentage varies depending on the tenant's particular business. Tenants such as supermarkets that have a high sales volume and low profit margin might pay no more than 1 percent in percentage rent. A discount department store may pay 2–3 percent while a fast food restaurant may pay as much as 6 percent of sales or more.

Percentage rent is determined by dividing the tenant's fixed rent by the percentage rent factor (expressed as a decimal). The resulting sum is the tenant's break point. When the tenant's annual gross sales exceed the break point, the tenant pays the landlord the agreed-upon rate of percentage rent on the excess sales only. *Example*: a supermarket agrees to pay $500,000 a year in fixed rent and 1 percent in percentage rent. Thus, that supermarket will pay 1 percent of its annual sales in excess of $50 million ($500,000/.01 = $50 million). So it will not pay any percentage rent until its sales reach $50 million. *Example*: a restaurant agrees to pay $200,000 in fixed rent and 5 percent in percentage rent; the restaurant will then pay 5 percent of its sales but only to the extent its sales exceed $4,000,000 ($200,000/.05 = $4,000,000).

An artificial break point occurs when the parties agree that, the formula aside, percentage rent will be payable on sales above an agreed-upon dollar amount. If the supermarket from the foregoing example agreed that percentage rent would commence above $40 million, then the artificial break point would be $40 million.

Triple net: The most basic of lease terms usually means that a tenant is required to pay its pro rata share of taxes, insurance, and maintenance and that the landlord is responsible for maintenance of the roof and outer walls.

Loan Terms

Basis point: a basis point is one one-hundredth (1/100th) of 1 percent. For example, 25 basis points are one-quarter of 1 percent, and so on. Basis points are often called *bips*.

Constant: the fixed payment of both principal and interest due under an amortizing loan. It is expressed as a percentage of the outstanding loan balance. The constant is determined by taking the total monthly debt service, multiplying it by 12, and then dividing that sum by the outstanding loan balance. The greater the principal amortization, the larger the constant. Older loans may have an attractive interest rate, but because so much of the fixed payment is principal, the cash-flow conscious buyer will object to the constant. *Example*: A $1 million loan payable in 30 years with interest at 8 percent has a constant of 8.8 percent in the first year. In the 15th year of the same loan, the constant has risen to 11.5 percent (the payments are unchanged, but are higher in proportion to the then remaining loan balance of $767,700).

Debt coverage ratio, or coverage: the ratio that a property's NOI bears to the annual principal and interest payments (or debt service) due under its loan. To obtain the coverage ratio for an existing loan, simply divide the NOI by the debt service. Example: if a property has an NOI of $125,000 and a debt service of $100,000, the coverage is called "1.25." If the NOI were unchanged but the debt service fell to $60,000, the coverage would be "2.08." The higher the coverage, the more conservative the loan.

To determine the maximum new loan for a property, you obtain the probable lender's coverage requirement and the new loan's constant. Next, you divide the property's NOI by the coverage ratio. Then you divide that result by the constant (expressed as a decimal). *Example*: The NOI is $327,000, the coverage is 1.15, and the constant is 8.8. Thus, ($327,000/1.15 = 284,348) /.088 = $3,231,225 maximum loan.

Leverage: A term meaning that a property is leveraged when it has debt on it. A 60 percent leverage means a property is encumbered with a loan for 60 percent of its value; being completely leveraged means the owner has no cash investment in the property.

Investors love leverage because it can exponentially increase their returns. If a buyer pays $1 million in all cash for a property that then appreciates $50,000 a year in value, the buyer makes 5 percent a year on the $1 million investment (on paper at least). If the buyer instead puts down $100,000 and borrows $900,000 from the bank, the $50,000 annual appreciation becomes a 50 percent return on the $100,000 investment. This is how the bold become wealthy in a rising market. Turning this example on its head illustrates what happens to them in a falling market. If—instead of appreciating—the property depreciates by $50,000 a year, then the all-cash buyer will suffer mild discomfort while the leveraged buyer will be in deep trouble.

Positive leverage: if the interest rate on the mortgage is lower than the cap rate, the buyer enjoys positive leverage. *Example*: If you buy a building for $1 million in all cash at a 7 cap rate, you will net $70,000 a year (a 7 percent return on the $1 million investment). If rather than paying all cash, you instead borrow $750,000, payable at 5 percent interest with a 30-year amortization schedule, you will pay $48,113 in annual principal and interest, but the cash investment will be reduced to $250,000. After debt service payments, you will be left with a net cash flow of $21,886—an 8.75 percent return on the $250,000 investment.

And you will benefit from annual principal amortization starting at $13,113 (and increasing yearly after that). If one counts principal amortization as part of one's return—and you should—then the overall return would be a handsome 14 percent.

Negative leverage: The reverse of positive leverage. It occurs when the interest rate on the loan is higher than the cap rate on the purchase price. If our buyer bought that building at a 4 cap, the NOI of $70,000 would be unchanged, but the purchase price would have soared to $1,750,000. If the buyer has the same loan, you will still have $21,886 in net cash flow, but instead of an 8.75 percent return on investment, you will receive 2.19 percent ($21,886 cash flow I $1 million equity). Buying at a 4 cap but getting 2.2 percent in cash flow is distinctly negative leverage.

About the Author

Malcolm Silver is the president of Malcolm Silver & Co. Ltd. His initiative, The Peace of Mind Real Estate Solution, is a simple and easy way to add real estate to investment portfolios.

Malcolm has more than twenty years' experience in the investment and financial services industries. Malcolm's real estate portfolio comprises properties that are underperforming at the time of acquisition, with a view to renovating and increasing rental values to market levels. His acquisitions are guided by a simple philosophy - buy run down commercial buildings in rising areas of Toronto, near transit.

His personal passion for real estate, encouraged by a long time family involvement, inspired him to package attractive real estate opportunities for investors. Malcolm is a Fellow of the Institute of Chartered Accountants in Ireland and has an MBA from INSEAD in Fontainebleau, France.

MALCOLM SILVER & CO. LTD
The Peace of Mind Real Estate Solution

Made in the USA
Charleston, SC
23 June 2016